The Elephant of My Heart

Jessica Clements

Illustrated by Simon McBride

BALBOA.
PRESS
A DIVISION OF HAY HOUSE

Cover Design/Interior Graphics/Art Credit : Simon McBride

Balboa Press books may be ordered through booksellers or by contacting:

Balboa Press
A Division of Hay House
1663 Liberty Drive
Bloomington, IN 47403
www.balboapress.com
1 (877) 407-4847

Printed in the United States of America.

ISBN: 978-1-4525-8572-7 (sc)
ISBN: 978-1-4525-8593-2 (e)

Balboa Press rev. date: 04/15/2014

Many thanks to my dear friend Teresa Pignatelli who introduced me to Isabella Ben Charrada who introduced me to "Mr Elephant". Many thanks to Stephen Gallegos, and the "Personal Totem Pole Process.

Thanks also to Simon whose drawings are inspirational. Thanks also to my proof readers my Mother, Liz Clements, Ruth Mateer. Also thanks go to Stephen Wish, Jan & Alex Prowse, Margaret & Roy Pugh, Greta & Colin Mattingley for their continued advice and support.

This book is dedicated to my Mother,
Elizabeth Clements

Prologue
by Stephen Gallegos

Thirty years ago I was given a great gift, a gift that began the reorganization of my life, of my being, of my presence in the world, of my thinking. The gift I received was that of the chakra power animals who arrived spontaneously and began the long path of healing to return me to the core of who I have always been. This experience of meeting the Chakra animals changed me and gave my life an entirely new direction. It initiated a return, a rebalancing, a realignment of who I am. I meet with the animals regularly and they entered me upon a healing path that was not only profound but also astounding. For most of those thirty years, I have also led others to meet and engage with their chakra animals for their own healing.

We can understand the chakra system as an alignment of aliveness, an alignment of energies that are core to our bodies. The chakra system is the nucleus of our wholeness. It is around this that the other remaining alivenesses gather themselves, and it is also the circle of our chakra energies that comes to govern our continued growing into wholeness. Our task is to remain in consultation with these energies as we grow and heal. We must earnestly befriend these energies and learn to care for and nurture our relationship to them. They are not our servants but wise and capable guides that move us step by step, passageway by passageway, toward our own wholeness.

In 2001, Jessica Clements met her Chakra animals in a journey led by one of my former students, Isabella ben Charada. For Jessica, the aliveness she found in her heart chakra, which came to her as Elephant, became a fundamental guide in her own journey to wholeness. In this book, Jessica Clements has shared with us all her journey with her Elephant of the Heart, exploring the guidance she received through this intimate relationship with her heart chakra and the deep healing, from a traumatic childhood injury, that occurred as a result.

Working within the layers of the Deep Imagination is the most powerful route to emotional healing, growing into maturity, and coming into balance with one's true being that I am familiar with. It is the avenue to our aliveness. Sadly, this is a way of knowing that we were taught, or encouraged, to abandon in childhood, thinking it childish whereas it is in fact the avenue to our wholeness.

In her work with children, Jessica guides them to meet their Animals of the Heart and subsequently works with them to create stage performances based on these experiences. In doing this, Jessica undertakes to foster and nurture a relationship with the deep imagination for these children and so generates essential pathways for them to connect with their own imagery and experience, and allows them access to their own balance and wholeness.

The deep imagination, is a realm that is not under our control. It is a layer that is significantly alive, that has its own direction and relationship with who we are. It is also the layer that can guide us back into our wholeness, for that is its job. Throughout historical time it has tried to do this in various ways. We have usually interpreted its presence as either religious or magical phenomena. Interpretation is our problem. The deep imagination was never meant to be interpreted. Instead, it is meant to be met directly and engaged with as a living element, having its own intelligence and its own purpose. To work with it, we need to form a companionship with it and allow it to guide us. In her book, Jessica Clements gives us a fine account of this way in action and delineates the healing and wholeness, our natural inner balance that returns as a result.

It is beautiful to see how Jessica Clements, grounded in her own personal experience with this work, is making it available to young people in a loving and creative way. Her Elephant of My Heart is a jewel of a book, to be treasured by young and old alike.

Eligio Stephen Gallegos, PhD
Author of The Personal Totem Pole Process©

Preface
Mum's Story

Dear Mummy & Daddy,

I know that if I don't scribble a few lines to you to-night, it will be next week before I find another moment to draw breath!

We've just had a very dramatic week here, with Jessica frightening the daylights out of us by getting viral meningitis!

Jessica was sent home from school last Tuesday and she really was very sick. When I consulted the doctor the following morning he immediately diagnosed meningitis. I just about had a fit on the spot. However like jaundice, there are two varieties – and she didn't have the lethal one. But she had to be very carefully watched & he dispatched me home with strict instructions to contact him immediately should any of a number of things he listed eventuate. Fortunately none did and she slowly recovered. Rest is really the only cure and patience! And that is what is running a bit thin at the moment. She thinks she can race around and read and play as normal – until the headache strikes again!! However today she has been considerably brighter and she is beginning to want to eat again and I think she is at last on the home straight!

Dear Mummy & Daddy,

I'm not sure where to begin but this is to fill you in on developments this end which, no doubts, Bill didn't have time to do on the phone.

Jessica has what is known as a cerebral aneurysm – a congenital defect in a blood vessel in her head. If it hadn't bled at this time they have assured us that it would probably have happened at another stage in her life. It is most unusual, however, in a child of her age.

Needless to say the symptoms are extremely distressing and since she is wired all over and being drip-fed I find sitting with her almost impossible. Bill so far has done most of this until this afternoon when I've been here for the past hour & a half and since she is quite heavily sedated she is reasonably peaceful and anyway Bill needed a break.

She was at first only semi-conscious but yesterday she recognised Bill and asked where she was. We see little change in her to-day but her neurologist told Bill to-day that her "lightness" was better, which in fact we've discovered means her level of consciousness is better. It's all highly technical but apparently they can tell by examining the optic nerves. When the sedation wears off she complains of desperate headache & is very restless and fretful.

Now for the outcome... the surgeon has explained to us that records show that there is no success when the operation is carried out whilst the patient is still in the acute stages. So, we must wait till she is back to normal – praying all the time that the vessel holds in the meantime & that there is no further leakage. He is pretty certain that the illness she had a few weeks ago, and which our local GP diagnosed as Viral Meningitis, was in fact the first warning of this.

The operation itself is a serious one – but we have no alternative. Almost certainly the vessel could leak again and in one of these she would die. Her neurologist was heartening though, and gave us a 90% chance of total success. If all goes well she should be back at school next term and able to lead a perfectly normal life again.

The Sister is a lovely person, and though careful not to give me false hopes, has been most helpful and encouraging. I, of course, am still in something of a turmoil, though stronger and more rational to-day than since it happened. I was so desperately upset when I first saw her that her doctor gave Bill some absolute "knock-outs" and it took most of Friday to drag myself out of the stupor. Since then our own doctor (who I might say, was also very upset that he hadn't picked it up the first time) has prescribed sleeping pills – but I'm trying to cope without them.

Dear Mummy & Daddy,
I had fully intended dispatching daily bulletins on Jessica but in the end found I couldn't concentrate sufficiently to write more than a couple of

sentences – and anyway by the time you got the letter the information would be so out of date that it would probably only have added to your worries.

It's now 2.30pm and we've just been to the hospital to see Jessica wheeled back from theatre & to see her surgeon. He assures us all went well – in spite of the intricacy of working within such a tiny space! It has to be done very slowly & delicately, which apparently is what takes the time. We saw her at 7am this morning before she went down to theatre – but she was really too dopey to take anything in & I doubt if she really appreciated that we were there.

With the feeling of "sitting on a time bomb" lifted I don't really know whether to laugh or cry! However we aren't completely out of the woods yet – and she may have to have another surgery – something known as a "shunt" if her blood pressure behaves erratically – as it has been doing during the past week.

I think I told you in my last letter that she will most probably have lost her sense of smell – but that really is a small price to pay for life! The other thing she will find hard to take, I think, is that she has had to be completely shaven – and her head is now bald! She always complained bitterly when I brushed it and often said it was too hot to have long again in the summer but could in no way be persuaded to have it cut. So I think she'll be in for something of a shock when she first sees herself. We will have to hunt around for a little wig and buy her a pretty sun hat to wear all the time.

We spent a very harrowing Saturday last, for when we went in that morning she had had what appeared to have been another slight "leak" – and she spent a very distressed and painful day – But we were cheered (and the doctors too) that at no time did she lose consciousness again. The nurses told me that they couldn't at anytime sedate her sufficiently to eradicate the pain for many of the drugs would prevent them being able to monitor the symptoms – and of course that was the only way they had of telling what was going on in her head. So for the past ten days she has had the mother and father of all headaches & a sore and stiff neck – the result we've since found out of the blood clotting at the top of the spinal column and producing immense pressure on the nerves.

I don't think that there is any hope she will be out of intensive care before Christmas & will then probably have to stay in the children's ward for some time too.

Dear Mummy & Daddy,

I shall try & scribble you a few lines tonight hoping that you might get it before Christmas though I doubt it, if it gets thrown in with the rest of the Christmas mail. Certainly if I leave it till Tuesday, there would be little hope of your getting it in time.

She made reasonably rapid progress till Saturday morning – though she was being fed large doses of drugs to help her cope with the pain & we were rather cheered – especially since the doctor said he hoped he might have her home in a fortnight! However on Saturday she suddenly started "drooping" complaining bitterly of pains in her head & neck and we discovered that all the drugs had been stopped & she was now having to "cope" on her own. She started vomiting again & generally became rather miserable and confused. We of course immediately "flipped" but everyone is still being most reassuring.

We were expecting too much too soon – she was being "carried" along by the drug therapy & sooner or later she was going to have to cope on her own – and they think since the drug dosage had to be so high, she is also suffering "withdrawal" symptoms, which to us seem like confusion.

So we will just have to be more patient & be pleased with a little progress every day, rather than expecting miracles. It was somehow such a relief when the operation was finally accomplished & apparently without damage, that I think we felt the tension would miraculously disappear!

Please thank everyone for including Jessica in their prayers – we have really been most touched by everyone's willingness to share our distress

& the support we've had from what seemed like every corner of the globe!

Our wedding anniversary, in fact, we told ourselves was our earlier escape to Sydney for two days. Nonetheless Eileen got to hear that it was the 16th and very kindly cooked us some Chicken in Cider & made some Paw Paw Salad and delivered it, frozen solid two days before. And we ended up eating baked beans & a rasher of bacon because I'd forgotten to thaw it in time!!

Anyway it was no disaster for we reckoned we'd been given our anniversary present the day before when we saw Jessica being wheeled back from theatre & able to manage a flicker of a smile at us!

I've been talking to the Sister about Jessica's operation & she tells me it is known as micro-surgery – for the vessel involved was so tiny that all the work had to be carried our using microscopes. And most brain and head surgery carried out whilst the patient is sitting on the knife-edge between consciousness & unconsciousness (therefore the anaesthetist's job is very important in this type of surgery) for all the time the patient's responses have to be checked. They lower the body temperature to a very low degree as well – which is why she was so icy when she got back from the theatre. She was like a disaster area – with no hair and a lurid scar across her scalp – and both arms black & blue from injections and drips – but she seldom complains – only of a headache & her sore neck!

We still haven't decided how we will find our Christmas Day. We'll probably all go to Church before taking Jessica's Christmas stocking over to the hospital. I hope by then she will have been moved to the children's ward and then the boys would be able to come in and see her too. In fact, they were allowed in very briefly today, but she didn't really register them for long – and made no comment about them even after they had gone.

We all send you lots of love and have a lovely Christmas, a big cuddle and a purr for Tara too from all of us. Jessica really misses Paddy & I think in a sense he is missing her too for he goes and sits forlornly on her bed sometimes as if enquiring where she is!

All our love,

Liz, Bill and the gang.

The Elephant of My Heart

My name is Jessica. I had a brain haemorrhage. That's like a bruise but in your brain. The problem with bruises in your brain is that there's no-where for the blood to go, so I got very sick. They had to do an operation on me to stop the blood vessel from leaking.

I should have got better but I didn't. My head began to swell and they had to do another operation on me. This operation put a plastic tube inside my head and then into my stomach.

Then I was taken back to my room in Intensive Care. This is where Mum said I would recover. It's a small room painted pure white with a large window overlooking a lake. I can't see the lake because I'm lying in bed. Mum and Dad have just gone out with a nurse to talk to the doctors. Mum did say they'd be back soon though.

That was when I heard the knocking on my door. I lay there wondering who was going to answer it. It continued and I waited. No one must have been able to hear it for they didn't answer it. I couldn't wait anymore. I decided that whoever was behind that door needed to be let in. I got up out of bed, and went across to the door. It looked a perfectly normal door into the corridor, but when I turned the handle and pushed open the door, there stood an elephant.

"Hello,' I said laughing. 'You're an elephant!' He stood quietly, gently swaying his trunk. 'But if he's an elephant,' I thought, 'how did he knock on the door?' The sensitive tip of his trunk swung up and wrapped itself around the metal doorknocker and promptly knocked again. 'But you understood what I thought?'

'Yes,' he said.

'You can speak!'

'Yes,' he replied, and he uncurled his trunk from the knocker and gently wrapped it around my waist. His breath was soft as he nuzzled the tip of his trunk into my hands. 'I am the animal of your heart.'

'Wow, you're the animal of my heart? I didn't know I had an animal of my heart!' I said excitedly.

'Yes, and if you climb up onto my back, I will take you to meet all your other animals.'

I wanted to say yes, but hesitated. I looked back at the bed and at my parents who were just coming back into the room. 'Can they come too?' I asked.

'No, this journey is for you alone,' he said.

'Will I come straight back, as soon as we've met all my animals?'

'Yes.'

'They will still be here when I get back?'

'Yes,'

'OK, but how do a get onto your back?'

I squealed as I sailed into the air. His trunk had tightened round my waist and up I had gone! He plonked me on the top of his huge head. 'Move back to my neck and put your feet down between my ears,' he said. I crawled back and found that my legs fitted snugly down between his ears.

'Wasn't that difficult?' I asked once there.

'What do you mean, difficult?'

'Well, wasn't I heavy?'

'No, you are very small and I am very big. You are easy to lift.'

I looked up as the elephant stepped into a forest of tropical green. There were huge trees hung with enormous plate-sized leaves. These took my eyes up to a tiny bit of blue sky between the tall, tall trees. 'Are you comfortable?' the elephant asked, sensing my movement.

'Yes, thank you.'

'Good,' he replied, 'I'm going to move now so hold onto the top of my ears.' My hands found the edges of his huge ears. They were like soft, crinkly pieces of grey paper, but warm. My hands gripped tightly for I was uncertain of just how my elephant would move.

He walked quickly through the forest. Though initially uncertain, so far above the ground on his back, I found my elephant's footsteps gentle. My eyes were stuck on the forest around me, and the birds that kept flying past, these I heard long before I saw them. Their cries were long, loud screeches. Turning towards this din I could see splashes of colour darting out from a dark spot amongst the trees. Then they'd be upon us, bright streaks of red, purple, yellow and blue across the green backdrop of the forest.

The elephant stopped. We were at the edge of a river. It was wide and shallow, running fast, dappled with white water and sunshine. He carefully walked into the centre of the river. 'You must not be afraid of this river,' he said, 'for it is yours. Its water is your life energy and into it you must go.' He sat down, rolled gently over and I promptly fell in.

I came up splashing! 'That wasn't fair,' I giggled. 'I didn't have a chance!'

'I know,' said the elephant, who wrapped his trunk around me and dunked me again. He brought me up out of the water and stood me upright on a little sandbank.

'I'm a drowned rat!' I said outraged. He stepped closer to me. 'You are not a rat, nor have you drowned. You are a little wet human with your hands on your hips,' he said, and his trunk gently nuzzled them off. 'On to my back again,' the elephant said, and I was soon sailing into the air to be placed ever so gently back on his head. I sat down, quickly grabbing the top of his ears as his huge body began moving underneath me. We walked out deeper into my river, to the sound of the chattering parrots and began walking down stream.

The river began to change. The sandy shores became banks as the water began to eat a gorge out through the earth. This didn't bother me for I was way up high on the back of my huge grey elephant. He was easily big enough and strong enough to manage a river of this size.

A large tree cut into the sky in the distance, huge roots coming out of the bank and arching into the river below. Its branches hung with fruit, like water dripping off wet hair. We stopped and my elephant lifted the tip of his trunk and picked one of them. His trunk curled up over his head, towards my hands. He squeezed it as he placed it into my hands, and they were covered with the juicy flesh. Giggling, I licked it as it dribbled over my hands. 'What are they called?' I asked.

"They are mangos,' he answered.

'Two more of these and I was getting full. It was then I saw and heard who else fed from this glorious tree. It was their fighting I heard first, then I saw them. Three tiny parrots wanting the same fruit. Each one of them certain it was theirs.

I began to laugh and saw that there were other branches with other tiny parrots having the same fight over similar fruit. They were bickering for the best spots, hanging upside down, wings spread to get the best position to feast on the delicious fruit. My laughter startling them, they were off, a tiny flock of them flying down the river.

"Oh, Mr Elephant, quick, let's follow them.'

'We have to wait here,' he replied.

'Why? Oh, please can we follow them? Please?'

'Do you remember that I am the animal of your heart?'

'Yes.'

'We have to wait because this is where we are going to meet another of your animals.'

'Which one?'

'The animal of your solar plexus.'

'My where?'

"Your solar plexus.'

'What's my solar plexus?'

'It's your second heart.'

'I didn't know I had two.'

'You don't, but it's easier to understand it that way. It's a large knot of nerves just below your heart.'

'What's it for?'

'It is for power.'

'Whose power?'

'Your power.'

'I think that it's easier to understand it as my second heart.'

'Yes, I agree. Now if you look very carefully at the base of your mango tree you will see her.'

'Where?' I looked. "I can't see her.'

'Look again.'

I crept forward onto the top of his head and stared at the bottom of the tree. Then I saw a movement under the leaves and roots. 'Is that her?' I squealed.'

'Yes, Do not be afraid. She will not harm you.'

It was then I saw her. She was a snake. She glided out from under the tree and showed herself in all her glory. She was like a moving carpet of shapes. Her head was flattened and painted with a diamond of sandy yellow, bordered with black. These shapes flowed down her long back, creating patterns of orange, yellow and green which caught the sun as she moved. 'Oh, Mr Elephant, she's beautiful!' I watched in fascination while she slid down onto the sandy shore and into the water. 'Is she coming this way?'

'Yes, she has a message for you.'

'For me?'

'Yes, for you.'

The elephant moved a little closer to the shore, stopped and waited. As the snake drew near he lifted his foot very slightly, helping her to coil herself round his foot. Having wound her length around the elephant's leg, with incredible speed she was in front of me on the top of my elephant's head. How she reached there so fast I did not see, but there she was in front of me, all curled in a perfect circle.

'Hello', I said, 'you're beautiful!' She certainly was. Her head rose above her body, while her two-tipped tongue investigated the air around her. She hissed.

"I'm sorry but I don't understand 'hiss'."

'Hiss.' The tongue emerged again.

'Don't you talk?' I asked.

'Hiss.'

I was confused. I had quickly grown used to my elephant talking to me. Needing time, I pulled my legs up from behind my elephant's ears, crossed them over and put my hands on my knees. I looked at the snake. Then I lifted the top of my elephant's right ear and whispered, 'Mr Elephant?'

'Yes.'

I know you told me not to be afraid, and I'm not, but I don't think Mrs Snake knows how to speak English, so what do I do now?

'You know that I am the animal of your heart?'

'Yes.'

'And that she is the animal of your solar plexus?'

'Yes, you said that was my second... my second...

'Heart. Do you know where the solar plexus is?'

'No'

'Then ask her to show you.'

'OK.' I let go of his ear. I grabbed it again, worried. 'It won't hurt, will it?'

'No. Do not be afraid; she is part of you. She is here to teach you who you are.'

I let go and tucked my feet securely down behind his ears. 'She is here to teach me who I am,' I repeated, hoping the idea would stick. I looked back at the perfect snake who still sat on the top of the elephant's head, watching me, tongue flashing. I took a deep breath, and said, 'Excuse me, Mrs Snake, Mr Elephant told me that you were the animal of my solar plexus...'

'Hiss', her tongue flashed again.

'Please would you show me where my solar plexus is?'

As soon as I had finished my question, her tightly coiled shape began to move. It was difficult to say where the move started, for the patterns of her head began to drop as her tail began to move. Her body was skilfully made for movement. Effortlessly she slid off the top of my elephant's head and very gently she moved towards me. I sat absolutely still, bewitched by her colour and shape as she moved. Her head, led by that double-tipped tongue, stopped just above my belly button. 'Is this where my second heart is?' I wondered, as my fingers found my skin closest to her. 'Hiss' was her only reply, as her diamond-shaped head moved through my fingers into my second heart. Her body was no longer in front of me; it was part of me.

My fingers touched the spot on my skin into which she had gone. 'Wow', I said, feeling her warm, soft skin pass my heart. 'She's tickling'. As these words left my lips, her head appeared at my mouth and out she came, her colours glistening vivid and true. Yet this was not all that had happened to my heart-felt animal, for she had changed like a butterfly from a caterpillar, and now she could fly! Her structure had grown wings and like an angel, she flew into the sky where she now belonged. 'Good-bye,' I called after her, but she was long gone, into the sky where the clouds sail and the parrots fly.

My elephant swayed gently, always careful of me.

'Will she ever come back?' I asked him.

'Whenever you need her she will return. All you have to do is ask. Now we must leave this place.' He began to move slowly into the river, away from the mango tree and the noisy parrots. I turned to watch the tree get smaller as I thought about what he had just said.

'If I asked her to return now, would she come?' My question turned me back to my elephant. He stopped walking. 'Do you need her now?'

I sat back, not expecting a question in reply! I sighed realising what my answer was. 'No, I don't think I really need her, but I want her to come back.'

'She is precious and, if you see her all the time, you will forget this.'

'Yes, I suppose you are right,' I answered, a little sadly.

'Are you ready to leave now?' he asked gently. I looked back at the mango tree, and the wondrous place we had just left, remembering the touch and taste of its fruit, and the animal of my second heart. I turned back to my elephant, lifted his ear and whispered, 'Yes, I'm ready.' And as we moved off, I turned back and watched it go.

Mr Elephant and I continued down the river. It was beginning to widen and run more smoothly. No more fast-racing shallows. The banks of the river were covered with plants and undergrowth. Some stood tall above the water, like a grassy fringe, and others sat with leaves wide, like brilliant emerald plates on the water's surface. My elephant kept close to the left bank. His pace was fast though, always smooth through this miniature jungle at the edge of my river.

Mr Elephant slowed and I began to catch a glimpse of who lived at the water's edge. All I saw at first were miniature greeny-blue darts. Then one landed on a plant as my elephant came to a stop. 'What are those blue, flying things, Mr Elephant?'

'They are dragonflies.'

'Do they look like dragons when they stop?'

'Look and see!'

I bent down over his left ear to get a little closer to these tiny dragons, watching them shoot past. One landed near the top of one of the tall grasses. Its body was long and thin and wrapped in the colour that was the blue of a peacock's tail. It was still too difficult to see any more of him so far up above the banks on my elephant. I lifted the edge of his ear, 'Mr Elephant, could your trunk get me down please. I'd like to get nearer them.'

'Then look on top of my head.' I shot back up and there sat a dragonfly. His body was bigger than it looked from above, but it was still that shimmering colour of the Mediterranean Sea. Its four wings were very delicate and transparent, except for a network of tiny lines holding them together like internal scaffolding. I gasped and he was gone. 'Oh, no he's off,' I squealed. 'If I say I need him, will he come back too? Please, Mr Elephant I have to ask if he's one of my animals.'

'Yes, he will and yes, he is.' My Elephant replied which stopped me talking for a few seconds as I tried to understand what he'd just said.

'Then why did he leave?'

Sit quietly and he will return.'

'I'm not very good at sitting quietly.'

'I know, but if you do, he will return.'

'OK, I'll try,' I sat looking at the back of my elephant's head, willing the lovely dragonfly to return. A while of this became a little boring, until I noticed what covered my dark elephant. He was covered in hairs. Not hair as in a human head of hair; there were never quite enough hairs to really be called that.

I wondered how many there were so I started to count. I had found a good little system. I pulled them down and tucked them under my arm as I counted them, ensuring they were never counted twice. I stopped at the thirty-fourth because sitting right beside it was the dragonfly. 'Mr Elephant, he's back', I whispered excitedly.

"Yes, I know.' he replied. 'Don't forget to say hello!'"

'Yes, oh, yes, OK. Hello Mr Dragonfly.' I waited. Nothing happened, so I went on, 'I never thought that dragons were beautiful, but you are, especially your colour.' I waited again for a reply. I sat some more. Having willed him back I was now willing him a voice. 'Perhaps you don't speak very loud.' Very gingerly, I put my face closer to where my dragonfly sat, so much closer that I saw his big, black pinhead eyes bulging off his head. They were saying nothing, or perhaps I just wasn't very good at reading them. I moved back, realising that Mr Dragonfly was not a good talker, unlike my elephant. Then I remembered what my elephant said I should ask when Mrs Snake wouldn't speak.

'Mr Dragonfly, if you can't speak, would you show me where in me you are from?' This done, I sat back and waited. The dragonfly moved slightly on his fine, thin legs, then he was up and off the patch of elephant skin like a helicopter, his body almost motionless above his launch-pad. He was hovering, his wings a blur. I jerked back as he moved like a jet towards my face. I sat transfixed by this tiny aquamarine dart, now hanging six inches from my nose. My curiosity was getting the better of me.

'Mr Elephant where in me is he from?'

'If you lift your head a little he will show you,' replied my elephant. Quietened, I did what I was told, as I was very curious as to what part of me this lovely creature was from and, of course, my heart wanted to know if she should prepare for another tickling!

'Not quite so far,' said my elephant. By this stage all I could see was the tropical blue sky and the very top of a nearby tree. I relaxed my neck, dropping my head so that my eyes could just see the aquamarine dragonfly start towards me.

His touch was quite definite, as if six tiny pencils had landed point first on my neck, though these tiny footprints melted into the purr of his wings. It was as if my trembling skin had instantly forgotten that his feet were there. Those moving wings I'd seen but never felt, he was giving to me; wing to skin. It stopped. I could no longer feel him on my neck. Only tiny aftershocks rippled through me. I sat there longer, stock-still, head slightly raised, caught in the memory of my dragonfly's touch, his kiss. I was upset. I hadn't wanted him to stop. I hadn't asked him to go. 'Oh, why did he leave?' I wailed, my head dropping sadly.

'He hasn't left,' replied my elephant.

'Yes, he has. I can't feel him anymore.'

'He is still there.'

'But if he's still there, why can't I feel him?'

'Just because you can't feel him does not mean that he has gone.'

'Then where is he?' My hand touched my neck and I found nothing; no dragonfly shape on my neck, no buzzing of his wings.

'He isn't here. He's gone just like Mrs Snake!' My elephant's trunk came up over the top of his head and curled round me. He swung me into the air and I landed in the river next to a couple of water lilies.

'Look at your reflection,' he said gently, as I stood knee deep in water.

The water took some time to clear after I'd been dropped into it! When it did, I soon found a little patch of water free from plants. I looked and through the last of the ripples, I saw the outline of my dragonfly under my chin. I bent forward, watching the faintest whisper of blue move into its thorax. I could not take my eyes off this insect on my neck as his true blue moved steadily into my reflection in the sun-speckled pool. Soon he was shining with all his former glory, emblazoned on my neck. His water-blue body was there, as were his four wings, each delicately tattooed in the tiniest of black lines. He was an amulet guarding my throat; my amulet of aquamarine.

'Oh Mr Ele, Mr Ele. He hasn't gone. Oh, look, he hasn't gone.' I lifted my throat to show him.

'No, he hasn't,' replied my calm elephant.

I put my arms around his trunk and gave my elephant a hug. 'Thank you Mr Ele Oh, dear,' I cried, pulling quickly away from him, 'is he still here?' My hand reached for my neck, terrified that I'd rubbed him off onto my elephant's trunk. I looked very carefully at his trunk, checking for hints of dragonfly blue on his grey skin.

'No, he is yours. You cannot rub him off. Check in the water again.' I did, and there he was still painted onto my neck in all his iridescent glory. Sheepishly I looked back at my elephant. 'Are you sure he'll always stay with me?'

'Yes.'

'So he'll stay forever?'

'Yes, or until you no longer need him and then you will ask him to leave.'

'Oh, I'll never do that Mr Ele. He's far too pretty for that.'

'Yes, his gift is colour. Yet when you grow up and see that shapes and colours are mere illusions you will no longer need him and you then will ask him to leave.'

Standing ankle-deep in water in front of my elephant I was still worried! 'But he is mine, isn't he?'

'Yes,' my elephant replied.

'And if I don't want him to go he will stay?'

'Yes, my little one, he will stay.'

'Great!

I turned back to my pool and as the water cleared, my hands found my dragonfly again. Yet my hand didn't hide my dragonfly, I could still see his outline and lovely blues through my fingers. No matter how much of my hand I put in front of my dragonfly, it did not stop me seeing him. 'Mr Elephant, my hand doesn't cover my dragonfly. He's still there.'

'Nothing will cover him from your eyes. He is there to protect your neck and your eyes will always be witness to that.'

'I don't understand.'

'Your eyes will always see your dragonfly protecting your neck. Nothing will ever hide him from your sight.'

'Not my big jumper that Auntie Bea gave me last Christmas?'

'No, you will be able to see him through that.'

'What about a suit of armour? It's impossible for anything to be seen through that!'

'Even that will not stop your dragonfly.'

'Wow, that's amazing! And he's mine, no-one can take him away from me?'

'No, nothing can. He is yours.'

'And if I die? Won't that take him away from me?'

'No, he will go to heaven with you.'

'Really? So nothing will ever take you from me, Mr Dragonfly, nothing.' I looked down at my reflection again, my fingers tracing the shape of my iridescent dragonfly, past his blue body, round his filigree wings, then over the tattooed dots of his black eyes. 'He is mine, he's mine, he's mine,' I kept saying over and again.

My reflection disappeared with my squirm of giggles. Mr Elephant's trunk had found my tickle spot! 'Stop that!' I squealed trying, unsuccessfully, to wriggle away. 'You can't tickle me now. You've moved my mirror. I was looking at my dragonfly!' But I couldn't stop laughing as his trunk circled round finding my other tickle spot, and then it tightened, lifting me skywards. I was then plonked very gently on top of my elephant's head.

I sat up looking around seeing the blue dragonflies darting amongst the flat water lilies and tall bulrushes at the edge of my river. The river ahead shimmered in the mid-morning sun and, as I took it all in, I knew it was time to leave. 'Mr Elephant, I'm ready to go now.' His trunk came slowly up over the back of his right shoulder and quietly he nuzzled it into my hands. "I am, Mr Elephant, really ready to go now,' I said stroking the tip of his trunk.

"Good,' he said, and away went his trunk as we began to move out into the middle of the wide river, away from the verge and grasses that held the beautiful insects that, like dragons, can fly. I didn't want to look back, but I did. I couldn't see exactly where we had stopped for the landscape all looked the same, and as I lifted my hand to the dragonfly at my neck I said, 'Good-bye.'

The river ahead looked very similar to that we'd left behind, just more of the same grassy banks. The few trees that dotted this savannah seemed far away and distant. The sun, as it continued to rise to its hottest point, made the waters shake with little heat shimmers. My elephant kept walking through the water, undisturbed by the effects of the rising temperature. I sank further into my seat between my elephant's ears and watched as the river moved hypnotically by. The warmth of the sun slowly worked its magic, and that with the rhythmic movement of my elephant soon lulled me to sleep.

I sat upright feeling myself slip. My elephant stopped, lifting his trunk to me. 'Are you thirsty?' he asked. My body moved, stretching itself out of its trance. 'Yes,' I said through a yawn. Then his trunk was beside me, dripping water into my hands. I drank the cool liquid, and went back for more. 'Thank you', I said my hands taking the end of his trunk and tickling it. 'Are you thirsty too?' I asked.

'Yes.' We stayed a while as he drank.

I settled back into my elephant's neck and noticed that now there were clouds in the previously clear sky. They were medium-sized clouds, not thin, wispy ones nor huge storm-clouds, though they were big enough to block the sun, and as they did, the colours of my river dulled. The sun's brilliance vanished as if someone had turned out the lights. My world was no longer there behind the cloud's shadow as my eyes slowly became used to the fading light.

As I refocused I found there were worrying nooks and crannies in parts of my river that were usually so bright and clear. Worried, my hands found the tops of my elephant's ears again and tightened their grip, for we had once again begun to move.

My world kept appearing and disappearing as the sun played peek-a-boo with the clouds. One moment every bulrush and lily pad stood fully lit and proud then along came a cloud and they merged into a grey-green khaki world of shadows.

'I wish the clouds would go away. I don't like them,' I said. 'Can't Mrs Snake fly back and chase them all away?'

'No,' my elephant replied.

'Are you sure?'

'Yes.'

'Why not?'

'Because if you chase away the clouds where will your next animal live?'

'My next animal lives in the clouds?'

'Yes, and if you chase all the clouds away he will have no-where to live. You will have destroyed his home just because it frightens you.'

'No, I wouldn't want to do that. That's unfair,' I answered looking up at the next cloud passing overhead. 'Is that cloud where he lives?'

'This you must ask him.'

'When will he arrive?'

'Soon.'

'How soon is soon?'

''Soon' just means more patience, my little one.'

'Patience. Oh dear. I'm really not very good at that.'

'I think you got to my thirty-fifth hair!'

'Oh yes, your hair!' I started counting again, but didn't get far! Knowing that my next animal was to come from the sky did not make the closeness of my elephant's hairs too interesting. My head kept turning upwards. 'I wonder, Mr Elephant, would you mind if I started counting clouds instead?'

'Not at all.'

'Thank you.'

I looked up and saw a stack of them marching across the sky towards the sun. I decided that there were three of them, even though I really couldn't tell if they were attached to each other or not. There was no blue sky between them, yet they were surrounded by golden edges that told me that the sun must have been able to get some way between them. There was a particular spark of gold that was not attached to the clouds. It seemed to have a mind of its own. It kept moving from one bit of the cloud to another, like a daytime shooting star. I watched as it swooped from cloud to cloud, realising it was getting closer.

'Mr Elephant?' I asked.

'Yes.'

'Is that my next animal?'

'Yes.'

'What animal is he?'

'Ask him.' I looked up and ducked for there, plummeting towards me was a large golden bird. His head was like an eagle's and his wings were huge canopies of gold, fire dancing off their feathers' ends. 'Wow! He is one of my animals?'

'Yes.'

'Wow! No. He can't be one of my animals!'

'Yes, my little one, see how glorious you are?'

"Am I?'

"Yes, you are.'

'Wow!' I ducked again as he hurtled over me, flying on towards the trees at the side of my river. He darted over their tops, disappearing into them to reappear as suddenly from their midst flying back towards me. As he neared me, he began to circle and climb. He then swooped down inches from the top of my elephant's trunk, stretching his wings out to control his speed, and came to a perfect landing on my elephant's head.

I was flattened on the top of my comforting elephant's neck, clinging to his ears and watching this creature's approach with awe. 'Are you alright Mr Elephant?' I whispered into the top of his left ear.

'Yes,' replied my unflappable, calm friend.

'Are you sure?' I asked.

'Yes, and now is the time for you to greet your newest animal.'

'I don't want to,' I replied suddenly overwhelmed by this, my newest animal. The tip of my elephant's trunk found my face.

'It is alright to be afraid,' he said.

'It is?'

'Yes, of course it is, but do not forget that I am here and will never leave you and that at your throat is your dragonfly.'

'Oh yes, my dragonfly.' My confidence was beginning to find her feet. I put my hand to my throat and sat up, and looked at this magnificent bird standing in front of me on my elephant's head.

'Hello,' I said, 'What type of bird are you? I asked.

'I am a Phoenix,' he replied. 'A golden Phoenix!'

Overwhelmed, I bowed, or tried to. From a sitting position this wasn't an easy manoeuvre. Yet bowing was all I could think of to do before this amazing bird.

'You bowed! How charming of you!'

'It was?'

'Why yes, of course it was, you silly little thing!' He moved towards me, turning to look at me out of his right eye. It was a very knowing stare. It did not, though, tell me anything about him. It said only that he could see straight through me! I laughed nervously. He turned his head and his left eye continued the stare.

'You are very handsome!' I said not knowing what to do or say.

'Yes, I am aren't I?' he said nonchalantly, rustling his golden wing feathers, letting off tiny sparks of light from their tips. I giggled. He was irresistible! 'May I touch you?' I asked, wondering what his golden feathers felt like.

'Why of course you may,' he replied.

Tentatively, I lifted my hand to his neck. I could see he was amused. 'You are laughing at me?' I said pulling my hand away.

'Yes, you are quite right. You are rather amusing! I mean do you really think that I - looking as splendid as I am - could be unpleasant to touch?' I sat back needing time to digest his words.

'I'm afraid that I've never met a bird like you before and I'm a little frightened. My elephant says that that's OK though!'

'Did he?'

'Yes, but just because you look nice doesn't mean you are nice,' I said beginning to find my confidence. 'There are some very pretty girls at school and they aren't very nice. They're horrible."

'You are wise, aren't you?'

'Is that being wise?'

'Yes, knowing that sometimes your eyes do not tell you all you need to know is an important thing to understand. Now young lady, I have an itch that needs to be scratched and you are just the little person to do that for me.' and he lifted his wing, his head held high, eyes closed expectantly, waiting for the scratch.

I looked at the huge expanse of gold stretching out around me and realised that I had no idea where to start. 'Excuse me, Mr Phoenix, where exactly do you want me to scratch?' He looked down at me. 'Under the fifth and sixth wing feather down!' I started to count. These feathers were lovely, strong and the colour of fire. I found the spot and delved between the feathers to find his skin, and there I began to scratch. He immediately started to coo. His skin was soft, and covered with the silkiest down I'd ever felt. As I scratched his head lifted and, satisfied, he closed his eyes. He then pulled his outstretched wings back and gave himself a complete body shake. I sat back, worried about getting caught in a shower of fire and light. Though I'd touched his feathers, I was not quite certain about what it would be like to be caught quite so close to a rain of gold.

'Thank you very much, young lady.'

'That's OK, Mr Phoenix. Have you got another itch somewhere you'd like me to scratch?' I asked.

'Well, now you come to mention it I have.' He lifted up his neck and said, 'Just below my chin is a particularly bad spot.' The feathers on his neck were much smaller than the ones on his wings, so his skin was much easier to find and I was soon scratching.

'Is this the spot, Mr Phoenix?' I asked, looking up him. He was transfixed with pleasure as I scratched the itch. Suddenly I felt something land on my hand and looking down, there was a very large flea. I took a closer look, pulling my hand towards my face. He was brown, had the usual six insect legs and his face was crowned with a pair of lovely long feelers. 'How do you do Mr. Flea. What part of me do you belong to?'

'My stomach!' interrupted my Phoenix, his beak bearing down on the flea. I pulled my hand away, not wanting my new friend to be eaten. 'I'm sorry Mr Phoenix, but he isn't big enough to be even a snack.'

'Yes, this I know, but that was not why I was going to eat him.'

'Then why were you going to eat him?' I asked.

'Because fleas are what make me itch so much!' I looked back at my flea, which had suddenly turned into two fleas.

'And they're very good at multiplying too.' He continued watching them with disgust. 'It really doesn't take long before you're completely covered with them.'

'Oh, I see. So you don't want these two back then?' I asked.

'No, young lady. They are all yours!'

'Thank you,' I said and I sat back looking at them, wondering where I was going to put them. I looked at my hand, aware that it wasn't covered with feathers as Mr Phoenix's was, it was just skin.

'Where do you think I could keep them?'

'In your hair?' suggested my Phoenix.

'Oh, good idea.' I lifted my hand into my hair and extremely carefully guided them onto my fringe. This spot was not to their liking for as soon as they'd landed on it they'd jumped back onto my hand again. They started going round in circles waving their antennae! 'Oh, dear, I don't think they like that as a home. I think they prefer feathers.'

'They might prefer feathers, but does the owner of the feathers prefer them?'

'No, you don't, I know! Are the itches very uncomfortable?'

'Why of course, especially when you can't scratch them!'

'That's what I'm here for though, isn't it?'

'Among your other charms!"

'Does that mean 'Yes' or 'No'?"

'It means that you give much more that just long-awaited scratches!'

'I do. What?'

'This I cannot tell you.'

'Oh, that's not fair! That's what Mr Elephant said.'

'Did he?'

'Yes, and he said that my other animals would tell me. Aren't you one of my animals?'

'Indeed yes, I certainly am one of your animals.'

'Then why don't you tell me?'

'Tell you what?'

'What I am! Or what I've done! Well, that's what Mr Elephant said you'd tell me.'

'He did, did he?'

'Yes he did!' My hands were on my hips, completely forgetting about their passengers.

'Watch out, young lady, Mr & Mrs Flea weren't expecting such a rough ride!' I froze looking down to see each flea still clinging to the backs of my hands!

'Whoops, I'm very sorry Mr Flea, I mean Mr & Mrs Flea.' As I spoke the right flea jumped off my hand and into the right pocket of my dress. I then saw my phoenix's left flea sailing off my hand and into my left pocket.

These were perfect pockets for them. They weren't the ones that slink at the side of a dress, hidden from the eyes of the world. These pockets stood like two square accessories to my dress. I looked inside the right one to check if Mr Flea was all right. It seemed that he was, because he'd duplicated. I watched as he became four then six and eight. I checked the left pocket and by the time I reached this one I couldn't count the number of fleas in Mrs Flea's pocket! I giggled, not really knowing what to do, as I watched my population of fleas explode! My pockets were beginning to be too small for them as they tumbled out and down onto my dress. From there, they didn't stop. They just kept moving out over my knees and down onto my elephant. They poured out of my pockets, this unending supply of fleas. These two ribbons of fleas continued down Mr Elephant's shoulders and out onto his legs, and on down to the reeds and plants that lay in the shallow water where my elephant stood. I couldn't move. I was too fascinated by what was happening.

'Now that really is a meal!' said Mr Phoenix.

I looked up to see him eyeing my fleas. 'You wouldn't really eat them, would you? They'd be very difficult for you to get into your beak. I mean if you were an anteater you'd have the right nose for insects!' I said.

'Yes, you are right. Nuisance they are; easy to eat they are not!'

'Good!' I looked back at them, still swarming out of my pockets. 'How many of them do you think there are?'

'Thousands I suspect!'

I put my hands gently on my dress below my pockets and felt the rush of fleas over them. It was as if I'd put my hands into a miniature stampede. I gently pulled them out and the few hangers-on jumped back into this tidal wave of fleas. 'There are so many of them!'

'Yes, fleas are very good at that.'

'At what?'

'Duplicating themselves.'

'Do you think they'll ever stop?'

'Yes.'

'Then what will happen? Will Mr & Mrs Flea follow their babies?'

'Yes, they will.'

'So they won't stay with me?'

'Does anything that's put in your pockets stay there?'

'I don't know, ' I said, suddenly uncertain.

'What? Doesn't your mother wash your clothes?'

'Yes.'

'And does the tissue or whatever it was you'd put in your pockets ever return?'

'No, Mum says I have to take out everything in the pockets before I put it into the wash.'

'Ah so you see, pockets are not places to set up homes in, not for Mr or Mrs Tissue, nor for Mr and Mrs Flea.'

'Yes, I see.'

I watched as the flea-numbers began to lessen. There were fewer and fewer of them following the crowd out of my pockets. The stream of fleas was tailing off, until there was but a thin line left. That stopped too as the last of the fleas decided to follow their kin. First came Mr Flea from my right pocket then as I quickly looked to my left pocket, I saw Mrs Flea start her descent. Down she went over my dress onto my elephant, down his leg and away. I bent over my elephant's neck to try to see her for as long as I possibly could, then she, her husband and the carpet of fleas they had created had gone.

I looked sadly back to my elephant's leg, then up to the back of his head where my Phoenix sat eyeing me with his right bead of an eye. 'Would you like another one? Believe me young lady I have plenty more!' His gold-plated claw lifted and a scratch began, which ended with a shake that sparkled with golden light. My hands went up, wondering if I could catch a sparkle of gold, but they fell through my hands like water. None caught, I returned to my golden bird. 'Thank you Mr Phoenix but I don't think so.' I paused.' Because if you did give me another, I don't think he'd stay either. I don't think they were ever meant to stay.'

'No, young lady, I think you are once again quite right.'

I smiled, remembering the avalanche of fleas foaming from my pockets. 'They were fun weren't they?'

'That's not my experience of them, but I am pleased it is yours.' I lifted my hand to touch his lovely gilt feathers again, watching as his down fell through my fingers leaving shadows and sunshine over my hand. 'What part of me do you come from?' I asked remembering that I did not know.

'I am from your brow.'

'My brow? Does that mean my forehead?'

'Yes, that is another name for it.'

'Wow, that's where you're from is it?' I raised my hand and placed it in under my fringe. 'No wonder Mr & Mrs Flea wouldn't stay there. They knew it was yours.'

'Yes.' He stretched out one of his wings and, tucking his head inside it, he started to preen. He stopped and after ruffling for a few seconds more through his wing he brought out a feather of gold. He looked at me, then holding out his feather, he dropped it into my hands.

'This is for you,' he said. I looked at this wonderful gift in my hands.

'For me? Are you sure?'

'Yes.'

'Thank you, thank you, thank you.' I wanted to hug him but didn't know how to hug a bird, especially one the size of my phoenix, so I sat, first looking at my solid gold feather then back to my fabulous bird.

'Now I must go,' he said. I stopped, eyes stuck on my feather. I said nothing, not even daring to look up at him.

'Are you sad, little one?'

'Yes,' I replied very quietly, my eyes still firmly on my feather.

'Don't be. You have part of me in your hand.'

'I know but it isn't all of you.' I looked up, 'You're fun. I love stroking and scratching your itches and…and you're lovely.'

He drew himself up; gold sparkled and shone from his feathers. 'Everything I am you are too, my little one. For I am the Phoenix of your brow, and all that is me, is in there in you.'

'So you're not going to stay?'

'No, if I stayed on the earth I would die. My home is the sky.'

'Where you chase sunbeams through the clouds and march rainbows out of rainstorms.'

'Why, yes, that is just what I do.'

'Then I have to let you go?'

'Yes.'

I sat looking at my feather, running my finger down its spine, teasing out the filaments and smoothing them back together again. It was entirely the colour of the sun, from root to tip. 'I will write to you with your feather as a quill,' I announced, understanding at last what a precious present I had been given. He stepped towards me and nuzzled his beak into my cheek.

I put my hands around him and gave him the hug I had wanted to give him earlier.

'Thank you for being so kind as to scratch those impossible itches."

'My pleasure,' I said entirely into feathers. I pulled myself out and looked up. "If you ever have any others I'd be delighted to scratch them for you.'

'Thank you, I will remember that,' he said starting to pull himself away. My hands followed his wings' retreat. They reached his tail and finally my Phoenix left my touch. He got to the top of my elephant's head and stretched his huge fiery wings; flames sparkled from every feather as he took off.

I watched as my magnificent phoenix circled the elephant, covering us both with golden light. He climbed away getting smaller and smaller as he soared out of the river basin and into the clouds from where he had come. I watched as he flew higher and higher, back to where he belonged, in the clouds. My sun-drenched bird had gone.

Mr Elephant lifted his trunk to my face and gently touched my cheek. I snuggled into it.

'Look what Mr Phoenix gave me.' I said quietly.

'What did he give you?'

'One of his feathers.' The sensitive tip of his trunk curled around it and took it to show his eyes. 'Isn't it lovely?' I asked.

'Indeed it is,' he said returning it to me, 'and what are you going to do with it?'

'I'm going to use it as a quill and write to him with it!'

'What a good idea,' answered my elephant.

'It writes in gold ink. Would you like some? I could colour your ears if you'd like me to.'

'Thank you. I would like that very much, but might I suggest you only paint the edges, as my ears are very large and you wouldn't have any golden ink left to write to Mr Phoenix.'

'Oh, yes, that's a good idea.'

I placed the nib of my feather on the ear nearest me. I started to draw the golden ink down the edge of his ear towards me. As my arm got to its furthest reach I knew I would soon have to lift the quill off. I didn't want to so I stopped at the furthest point I could reach. A wobble shook my quill off but to my complete surprise, the ink didn't stop. It took off at a gallop, charging down the edge of his ear until it was out of my sight. I stretched up hoping it was going to circle my Elephant's ear and it did. There it was shooting up the other side. I leaned as far forward as I could, clinging onto the other ear, to see the lines meet. And as these two bands met they set off a glorious ripple of gold round my elephant's ear.

"Wow. You should see what's happened. You've been 'engolded!'" I said.

'What a lovely thing to be,' replied my elephant.

'Now for your other ear." I turned to the other one. This time I wanted to see clearly where the lines of gold met. So I put my feather at the center of the top and very slowly started to draw the glistening gold towards me. I stretched as far as I could down my elephant's left ear and then I had to let it go. As I did, I pulled myself quickly up to see the gold I'd left below shooting up the other side sending pulses of gold round my elephant's ear.

'That was brilliant, Mr Elephant. Are you sure you don't want the whole of your ears gold?'

'Yes, I'm sure. My colour is grey.'

'So you don't want any other bits of you gold then?' I asked. He lifted his trunk and nuzzled my hands. 'What about the tip of your trunk?'

'I would be honoured to have a golden tip to my trunk', he replied.

'Oh, great. This will take me ages!' I tickled the tip of his trunk with the soft end of the feather till he started snuffling at me. Laughing, I turned my feather round and started to paint. I drew all the way round the edge, then sat completely absorbed as I filled in the colour. The last bit completed, I sat back to view my handiwork. 'Take a look!' I said. His trunk slid away for inspection. It soon returned and nuzzled my cheeks. 'Isn't it lovely?'

'Yes, indeed it is. Thank you very much for my gold. I will wear it with pride!''

He took his trunk down and began to move again. The riverside ahead was changing. Gone were the reeds and water lilies. They were replaced by drifts of sand.

I watched them slide by as we strode past them. The jungle had returned. A far-off backdrop of jungle-green bordered the outer reaches of the sandy edges of the river. Those beaches looked warm and inviting, patterned by the river's flow. I wanted to get down.

'Can we stop please, Mr Elephant? I'm getting a bit tired.

'Yes, of course.' He turned from his path through the middle of the river and we waded towards the nearest sandbank.

'Are you getting tired too?'

'Yes, a little.'

Once at the beach, his gold-tipped trunk wrapped around my waist and I was back sailing through the air. He placed me gently on the beach. 'Thank you Mr Elephant.'

'You're welcome.'

Once I'd unwrapped myself from his trunk, excitement replaced tiredness, and I scampered off to explore this new world. I dug my bare feet into the sand and watched them disappear into a perfect sand-fill. I hadn't been on the ground with water round my ankles before and it was fun. 'Look at me, I'm shrinking,' I shouted in mock horror.

Mr Elephant was no longer where he should have been! He'd shrunk too. He had lain down on his side with his huge feet stretched out in the sand. This was frighteningly new to me and I pulled my feet out of my sand fill and raced over to him. 'Are you all right?' I called as I ran. His trunk found me first and wrapped itself round me, squeezing me carefully. 'Yes, I am. Thank you.' I looked into his milky white eyes. 'You must be really tired you're lying down.'

'I do need a short rest.'

I looked at his huge white tusks from a new angle. They were dirty with bits of mud and foliage from our trek through the day. I ran my hands over them feeling how straight and true they were. 'I will wash your tusks,' I decided.

'How kind of you,' he replied.

I stood back and took a long look at his tusks. They were enormous, bigger than I was, and I soon saw that the little splash of water I could hold in my hands would never wash them. I needed something larger that would hold more water.

'I'm just going to get something to help me wash your tusks, Mr Elephant.' Going down to the water's edge I found a leaf. It was a large water-lily leaf, flat and circular. I fashioned it into a cup-shape and tried it out. Apart from a few drips it was perfect. I rushed as fast as I could through the sand back to my elephant. I poured the water over his top tusk and rubbed its length, removing the greenery and mud. A few more of these 'leafuls' and both his tusks were clean.

"Mr Elephant?'

'Yes'

'Your tusks are lovely and strong.'

'Yes, indeed they are. Thank you for cleaning them for me.'

'My pleasure.' I sat down and looked at his feet and saw his huge toenails. They too were dirty. I crawled around them wondering if his feet needed attention. They did, for there were many stones caught between his nails. "Ouch, Mr Elephant. You've got so many stones stuck in your feet, don't they hurt?'

'Yes, sometimes they do.'

'Would you like me to clean and wash them too?'

'That would be very kind of you. Thank you.'

I began the task of removing the stones from between his toes, but some were too deeply embedded. 'I'm afraid Mr Elephant, that I can't get them all out, I need a stick to help me.' I got up. 'Won't be a sec'. I'll try and find one.'

I scampered off down towards the river. My search wasn't very productive. There were small stones, flat and worn by the river, and a few other leaves but no sticks. I headed towards the trees then stopped. I turned back to look at my elephant. These trees seemed a long way away from him. I'd never been away from him in my new world. He'd always been with me. I looked again at the forest. It looked miles away from my resting elephant, so I turned and scampered back to him. This was somewhere I wasn't ready to go!

As I got to him, I remembered his feet. I got some water in my water lily leaf-cup and sat down in front of one of his front feet and started to wash. As I was brushing my hand down his foot, my fingers found a large stone lodged deeply between a toenail and the edge of his foot. I pulled at it trying to gouge it out. He winced, and pulled his foot away.

I sighed. If I wanted to manicure my elephant's feet properly I needed to find a stick! I looked up at the green outer reaches of my sandy beach and knew I had to go.

'I'm just going a bit further to look for that stick,' I said getting up. Cautiously putting one foot in front of another I started to leave the closeness of my elephant. "He needs to have his feet cleared of stones. He needs to have his feet cleared of stones." I kept saying to myself as I trod purposefully towards the jungle. My footsteps quickened as I strode out wondering how long it would be before I found the stick I was looking for.

And there it was! It was a small, sun-bleached stick with half of one side of it broken off making a sharpish point. "I've got it,' I yelled running back to my elephant. I sat down next to his foot and with a deep breath began very gently to prize out the large stone.

As well as stones there were thorns that had become embedded in his flesh. They came out easily though they worried me because they bled. 'Won't be long,' I hollered as I rushed to the river and brought back fresh water to wash away the blood from his tiny wounds. After my third trip for water I went round my huge elephant's legs back to his face to check that he was all right. 'Does it hurt when I pull out the thorns?' I asked.

'Not once they are gone,' he answered.

'Are you sure, because they bleed such a lot, and I don't want that to hurt.'

'You are a kind and careful 'thorn-puller', and I'm very grateful that they are gone,' he answered.

'All right, if you're sure.' Once again I returned to my job.

I got to his left back foot and had just poured another leaf's-worth of water over him when I began to see that my elephant's foot was no longer an elephant's foot. He was changing from being grey to being black, and from being hair-covered to being fur-covered. I watched as his foot became smaller and as his huge toenails began to sharpen, retracting into sheaths of black fur. His legs shrank as my eyes chased his transformation up his legs throughout his body. His ivory tusks and gold-tipped trunk vanished into whiskers of grey and the all-knowing eyes of my elephant melted into the unsaying-eyes of a cat. My gigantic elephant had gone and there in his place lay a black panther. I sat stunned. He was magnificent.

He rolled onto his back, stretching lazily, his green eyes never leaving mine.

'Where has my elephant gone?' I asked very cautiously.

'I am your elephant.' His voice was soft, strong and very low. It was as if he was roaring and purring at the same time.

'But you're not an elephant, you're a cat.'

'Yes, I am the panther of your heart.'

'But I thought my elephant was from my heart."

'He is.'

'Then how can you be from there too?'

'I am the strength of your heart, and you have a strong, strong heart.'

'I do?'

'Oh yes, you certainly do.' He lifted his front paw and placed it very carefully, claws still firmly sheathed, on my chest.

'My heart!' I whispered. I began to fall over, as his touch became a push. I laughed as I hit the sand and was soon being sat on by the panther of my strong heart. 'I can't breathe,' I said,

'So if you can't breathe, how can you speak?'

'All right. I was joking, but you are heavy and....' I stopped I didn't know how to tell a large black cat sitting on top of me that I was getting scared.

'Are you frightened of me?' inquired my large black panther. 'How can you be frightened of your own heart?'

'But, you're heavier than I am and you are squashing me, and anyway, why can't I be frightened of you?' I blurted out, and promptly regretted it. He got off and sat down beside me in the pose of an Egyptian cat statue and one that rumbled! I sat up and looked at him. 'Are you purring?' I asked curiously.

'Yes,'

'It's not like a cat's purr, is it?

'Doesn't that depend on what you class as a cat?'

'You are like my elephant!' I answered remembering my elephant's ability to answer a question with a question.

'I am your elephant!' he said, dropping his head down to my level and ever so gently our cheeks touched. I couldn't work out if it was his cheek that was stroking mine or if it was mine that was stroking his.

'This is cat kissing, isn't it?' I remembered how my cat, Paddy, would greet me with his hungry early morning cheek rub. 'My Mum calls this puppy love!'

'I see,' said my panther obviously annoyed at being likened to a dog.

'Well, what about panther love?' I giggled.

'A little less frightened, are you?'

'Yes, lots less frightened.'

'Good, now we can play!'

'Play? Yes. What shall we play?'

'Panther play!' and he galloped off. I ran after him, panting and giggling at the same time.

'Come back. You're faster than I am!' He circled around me and pounced.

I darted out of the way, but my panther was right behind me and I felt paws encircling my shoulders. I tumbled to the ground, just managing to remove his big, black paws.

Back upright I crouched and jumped out of his way turning to see where he was going next. There he was, cool as a cucumber, sitting, once again, like an Egyptian cat statue. I watched him, wondering what he was going to do next. I could hear him purring, 'You're purring, but I don't think you're offering 'panther love!' I said. I wasn't a fool. He landed on top of me, knocking me backwards into the sand, and his tongue, rough and wet, began to remove every last particle of dirt and what seemed like skin from my face. 'Err, yuck, that's ... yerck,... er stop that!' I said, pushing him away - but every shove and push I gave he countered, moving so expertly that I had nothing to push against. At the same time I was trying to get up, which he soon stopped by sitting firmly on my legs. I sat with my hands dug deep into the sand behind me trying to keep upright.

'Thank you. That was horrible!'

'Was it not 'panther love' you wanted?' he enquired, eyes twinkling. 'Is not love a thorough wash?'

'No, it isn't! Maybe a kiss or a hug but a wash - yerck!"

'Perhaps you are too young!'

'Look, I'm not too young at all. I'm nine and three-quarters which is very old.'

'So I see!'

Delicately, he got off my legs and brought his face close to mine. He was impossible to resist, his fur was so black and soft to the touch. I put my fingers under his chin and stroked his lovely neck. He purred again. 'Ah, ha, you see, I know exactly where you like to be tickled!' I said, as his chin rose as I stroked him and his purrs began to deafen me. He was coal black and his fur had a moonlit sheen. His whiskers sat proud and noble at his muzzle. I ran my finger down his smooth black nose. 'You are so, so lovely.'

'As are you, young lady!' His eyes shot me a playful look and he darted away from me.

'Oh no I'm not!' I hollered scrambling up and running after him. As I got near to him he stopped, turned and jumped. I watched him sail over my head landing just beyond me and then he scampered off.

'Come back here!' I screamed, chasing him. He wasn't running fast but just quick enough for me not to be able to catch him. I panted after him still determined to catch him. He led me this way and that, then spun me in circles until I could go no further. I sank to my knees taking huge gulps of air. He sat down and waited for me to recover – and then he pounced.

I felt him pass over me, missing me by inches. Lithely he turned and sat down. He was sitting with all four paws hidden underneath him. I put my arms around his strong and powerful neck and lent against his soft, black shoulders, hugging him. 'I've got you,' I said giggling, knowing how wrong I was.

'So you have!' he said, and rolled over taking me with him. One front paw came up between my hands and I hung onto his fur as the force of his turns took me spiralling round. I couldn't hold onto his shoulder for much longer as we spun across the sand. Eventually scrabbling to hold onto him my hands slid down his cheek. With a yelp, he jumped away and sat poised and uncertain, watching me.

I looked down and there in my hand was one of his dark, black whiskers. I couldn't remember how it had got there. I knew I hadn't pulled it out, yet the skirmish had been such fast and furious fun that I really couldn't recall exactly what had happened as I'd clung desperately on. 'Oh, dear! I'm so sorry, Mr Panther, I didn't mean to take one of your whiskers. I really didn't,' I said anxiously.

'I know.'

He sat down, and started to wash his face. He closed his eyes while his very pink tongue wet his black paw. He then lifted this soggy paw to the top of his black muzzle, and dragging it down he washed his nose. He repeated the procedure on the other side of his face. I walked slowly over to him and stood next to him fascinated by his washing.

'Will you do that to me?' I asked, wondering what it would feel like.

'That was not what you said last time.'

'Oh, yes, that's true,' I said, as I remembered his rough, wet tongue sand-papering my face.

'What are you going to do with my whisker?' he asked.

'I don't know. I can't put it in my pocket because nothing that I put in there ever stays, so I don't really know where I can put it.'

He nuzzled his long, black muzzle into my chin finishing with a lick on my nose.

'It's still yucky,' I laughed as my hand ran down his silky fur.

Then I felt a soft tingling at my throat. 'Mr Panther, I think it's Mr Dragonfly,' I said. very excited. The tingle became a whir as my dragonfly began to emerge from my outstretched neck.

'Place my whisker onto the palm of your hand and give it to your dragonfly,' said Mr Panther.

'He'll keep it for me then?' I asked as I started to feel my dragonfly's feet, needle fine, moving off my skin. Then he was away, like a miniature helicopter up off his position guarding my neck. We watched as the blue dragon jetted off around us.

'Give him a landing pad and don't forget my whisker.'

I lifted my hands with the strong, black whisker laid across them and waited. The dragonfly darted here and there, and we waited some more. Then he was there on my hands. He sat washing his antennae, then he was off again heading straight for my throat. 'He didn't take it,' I said panicking.

'I don't think he could. He is small and my whisker is big. Why don't you give it to him at your neck.'

I could feel the air moving round my throat as the dragonfly returned, his six little feet landing on my neck. I lifted the whisker and inserted it between his feet and my skin. It was then my dragonfly got to work. He stitched my neck with the panther's whisker. His legs were the needles and my skin the silk cloth. His tiny legs worked hard, lacing the fine, strong whisker through my soft skin. He knew what he was doing though and soon there was no whisker left, just the finest stitches. The wound had gone!

So was my panther. My elephant's trunk nuzzled into my chin. 'Hello Mr Elephant. Where's Mr Panther?'

'I am your Panther.'

'Oh no, he said that he was you, too. Why can't I have both of you here with me at the same time?'

'You have, silly. I am he as he is me.'

'I don't understand!' I wailed.

'You will, little one,' and I was lifted into the air again by his lovely golden-tipped trunk. I crawled back to my spot between his ears and slumped down. I was annoyed.

'Why did he leave without saying good-bye?'

'He did not need to say good-bye.' I didn't reply.

'Did I say good-bye when I changed into Mr Panther?'

'No, you didn't!' I replied, still annoyed.

'Because I was still there. I am Mr Panther. He did not say good-bye because he has not left you. For he and I are one.'

I put my hand to my neck and felt for my dragonfly and whisker. I could feel the slightest tremor of Mr Dragonfly's wings and I could faintly hear the rumble of my Panther's purr. The gentle swaying of my elephant brought me back to him and I remembered his newly-washed feet. 'How are your feet, Mr Elephant?' I asked.

'Fine now they are cleaned. Thank you.'

'I'm sorry I got angry Mr Elephant.'

'That's quite all right. You thought you'd lost something precious, and that always makes one feel unhappy and cross.'

'I haven't lost him, have I?'

'No, little one. He's always in your strong, strong heart.'

'Good.' What shall we do now, then? What animal have I yet to meet?

'You have one more animal to meet.'

'Just the one?'

'Yes,' my elephant replied.

'What part of me does he belong to?'

'This you must ask him.'

'Where will we meet him?' I asked.

'Underwater,' replied my cryptic elephant.

'Under water? Will I be swimming?'

'No, but you will be covered with water.'

I sat back thinking about what my elephant had just said. We had begun to walk again, out into the river, now swift and shallow again. The water tumbled past my elephant's newly washed feet. I wondered what type of animal I was next going to meet. The banks of the river bent into sandy banks then returned to jungle. Dark green trees covered with vines hung over the river covering it with dark shade. I was no longer afraid of these shady spots for I knew the Phoenix would bring them light if I wanted it.

We moved quickly and quietly through the bubbling water till I saw a huge bend in the river. We stopped before it and my elephant lifted up his trunk and gently touched my face.

'Is this where we're going to meet my next animal?' I asked very excitedly.

'Yes, but first you need a bath!'

'Oh, no not again!' I squealed.

'Yes, but the water has a job to do.'

'What job is that?'

'Each droplet takes something from you as it runs over you.'

'What does it take?'

'Your fear.'

As he said this, his gold tipped trunk left me and he filled it full of river water. Lifting it he shot a plume over his head. My hands out-stretched, my eyes closed waiting for the water I knew would soon be covering me. I felt the weight of it hit. My eyes opened as its speed slowed and I saw that it wasn't water that was cascading over me, it was liquid silver that ran down me and my elephant. Touching the grey of my elephant it shimmered down his wrinkles in streams of light metallic silver. I held out my hand to catch some but it had ideas of its own and fell through my tightly clasped fingers.

'I can't catch it!' I hollered to my elephant. His trunk went back into the water and I was again showered with this liquid steel. It didn't want to stay and slipped speedily down us only to be replaced by more from my elephant's gilded trunk.

I had stopped counting how many elephant-powered waterspouts fell on me so that, when it did stop it took me some time to catch my breath. I opened my eyes and found a drop of silver-water at the end of my nose. It hung there suspended as if by magic. I crossed my eyes to get a closer look and saw, in its middle a goldfish. I sat very still not wanting to disturb him. 'Hello, Mr Goldfish, are you the animal of my nose?'

'No, of course not. I am the animal of your roots. Now will you put me back into my river!'

'I see. Well, yes, of course I will,' I replied not really knowing how I was going to get him down. 'Excuse me, Mr Goldfish, how would you like to get down? 'I could lift you on to my elephant then you could slide down his side and into the water,' I said.

'What me? Slide down this elephant's back? Oh, no, no, no! That simply will not do!' replied my self-possessed little golden fish.

'Well, the only other way down, is if I lift you onto my finger and hang you out over my elephant and drop you directly into the water!'

'That sounds infinitely preferable,' he answered.

'Yes, but you might get hurt in the fall.' I was worried about what might happen to my newest animal.

'No, I won't! Now will you get me down.'

Motivated into action by the sheer force of this tiny personality I delicately placed my hand under the drop still hanging from the end of my nose and gently felt the warmth of the droplet touch my palm. A flicker of movement hurried me as my fish impatiently moved his tail and fins. I leant out as far as I could, holding the gilded edge of my elephant's ear in the other hand and, turning my other hand over, I let the golden fish within the silver droplet fall.

Down it fell into the water. I watched it go sadly not thinking I'd see it again. As it hit the water I saw how many other goldfish were swimming in the river below us. 'Look Mr Elephant, there are hundreds of them.'

'So I see."

'Can I get down, Mr Elephant, please! Please can I get down?'

I scrambled on to the crown of his head and saw his trunk waiting for me. He curled it round me and I was carefully placed into the water.

'Thank you,' I said, quickly leaving my elephant's trunk as my attention was taken by this gilt-red sea at my feet.

I had been wrong. There weren't hundreds of these fish, there were thousands. My river was red with them. I very gingerly lifted my feet to try and walk and felt fishes everywhere. They were smooth and soft and very fast. My foot found the ground and I started to walk. Everywhere there were flashes of gold and red. As soon as I moved my eyes to look at one, I'd see another beckoning and away my eyes would go.

'Where do you think they're going in such a rush?' They were all swimming towards the bend in the river. I looked back at my elephant.

'They do seem in a great hurry.'

'Perhaps that's why my goldfish wanted to get down so fast?'

'Yes.'

'Can we go with them?' I asked cautiously, not knowing what my elephant would say.

'Yes. Would you like to ride on my back?'

'No, I think I'd prefer to walk with them.'

'Good.' He nuzzled his trunk into my giggle-spot, making me laugh and we began to walk. The fish parted as we stepped through them as we walked down our river.

Our progress was slow. My stride was much smaller than my elephant's but we gradually got closer and closer to seeing where it was these fish wanted to go. But as I saw where they were going it stopped me dead. One side of my river had soared into a cliff and into that my river ran. A dark, black cave sat at the bottom of this sun-whitened rock face. I pulled my elephant's trunk close, frightened by what I saw. I didn't want to go any nearer.

'I don't like this,' I whispered.

'Can you remember what I said to you when I showered you with your river-water?' My elephant asked as I crept behind his trunk and under his tusks. I was tucking myself well in behind my huge, grey shield. 'Can you remember?' he repeated very gently.

'Yes,' I whispered.

'What did I say?' he asked again, carefully coaxing the answer from me.

'You said that every drop that rolled off me would wash my fear away.'

'Good. And do you believe that?'

'Yes. I think so.'

Then what is it that frightens you now?'

'The cave.'

'What is it about the cave that frightens you?'

'It's dark.'

'Is it?'

'It looks dark!'

'Just because something looks dark doesn't mean it is dark.'

'Yes, I know, but ...'

'Wasn't that what you told your Phoenix?'

'No, I don't think I said that!'

'But you said that just because girls looked nice didn't mean they were nice.'

'Is that the same?' I asked too frightened to be sure.

'Yes, sometimes things are not what they seem to be.'

'So the cave isn't dark?'

'Shall we find out?'

I very carefully poked my head out from under his trunk and looked at his huge, gentle eyes, and touched the golden tip of his trunk that was threading through my arms.

'You will never leave me, will you?'

'No,' my elephant replied.

The cave no longer seemed so overpoweringly dark as I remembered the silvery water rolling all my fears away. 'OK, let's go!' And I marched off in the direction the glorious golden fish were taking me, towards the cave.

As it approached I began to have second thoughts. 'Are you sure it's OK?' I asked, creeping close to him again.

'Nothing in life is without fear. But it can be lessened if you remember that nothing is as it seems.'

'I think I understand,' I replied uncertainly.

'If you put your hand into the water and take it out again, what happens to the water on your hand?'

'It runs away.'

'Back into the river from where it comes. So too with your fear if you see it for what it truly is.'

'So if I see the cave as it truly is I won't be frightened of it?'

'Yes. '

'Does this mean that I have to go into the cave?'

'Yes, for it is only when you are there can you see it as it truly is.'

I looked back at my thousands of goldfish and watched them fearlessly stream into this cave. 'I suppose if they aren't frightened of it then why should I be?' I said encouraging myself. We began to walk slowly towards the mouth of the cave.

The darkness of the cave got blacker and blacker. It was the colour of my panther but without his sleek shine. It was a dull black. We got closer and closer until we were at the rocky entrance itself. We were still bathed in sunshine for it shone a little way into the cave catching the golden reds of my fishes under our feet. Yet this made the darkness beyond even blacker. 'Can I hold your trunk please, Mr Elephant?' The tip of his trunk had found my hand as soon as I'd said it. 'Thank you!' I whispered as we walked out of the light and into the depths of the cave.

My sight left me as I walked out of the sunlight and into the darkness. The blackness seemed to cover everything as I slowly edged forwards, tightly holding my elephant's trunk. My feet kept reassuring me that my river was the same, still shallow and cool. The golden reds of my fishes sifted through the blackness of my vision. 'I can still see my fishes', I whispered excitedly to my elephant and as I lifted my head to speak I saw sparkles of red darting up from my feet to the walls of my cave. 'They're climbing the walls! They're all over the place.'

I stopped and watched as the reds were followed by deep blues, emerald greens and lastly a brilliant white. This feast of colour flashed and twinkled, surrounding us with a dazzling underground firework display. My eyes couldn't keep up with it all. A shaft of blue took my sight upwards followed by a twist of red. Then a streak of green dragged my eyes back down the other side of the cave and disappeared into the vast bulk of my elephant. I ducked under his trunk to find out what colour was behind him.

'What are they?' I asked as I watched quite bewitched by the magical colours.

'They are gemstones.'

'Gemstones?' I said. Letting go of my elephant's trunk. 'Are the blues sapphires?'

'Yes. And the greens are emeralds, the reds are rubies and the twinkles of white are diamonds.' He lifted his trunk up to the top of the cave where a cluster of reds glowed. The tip of his trunk found the deepest of reds and took it from its bed of rock then placed it on top of his head.

'Let me see, let me see, please, please let me see it,' I squealed excitedly. My elephant caught me in his trunk and I was on his back in front of this wondrous gem.

The ruby was as large as my hand and it glowed the deepest of reds, its centre burning with a deep, inner fire. My elephant then turned and started to move out of the cave. As the light caught the stone I saw a glimpse of my goldfish moving through the facets of this magnificent gem. And he was gone. I looked down wondering if the fishes were still below me but they too had gone. Mr Elephant turned and we left the cave.

I looked up at the cliff past which my elephant strode and saw parrots clinging to the sides of it, furiously chattering away. Their colours reminded me of the gems in my cave. The ruby my elephant had put on his head glinted in the sunshine. 'Thank you Mr Elephant. I'm no longer frightened of my cave.' I turned back to see it once again. 'Good-bye Mr Goldfish' I shouted at the top of my voice.

Where was Mr Goldfish going Mr Elephant?' I asked.

'Wherever he wants to go.'

'Do you think we could come back here again someday?' I asked.

'Yes.'

We had begun to walk back round the bend in the river and as we did so I waved goodbye to my sparkling cave. I watched as we passed the sandy banks cutting into my shallow river. I laughed remembering my sleek black panther and our play-fights. My hand touched my throat where his whisker lay as I heard again his thundering purrs.

We were moving quickly, now, down my riverbed. The sky around us was suddenly dimmed as a cloud took the sun from us. I watched again as my world disappeared into dimmer shades of green. I looked up at the gold-rimmed clouds, remembering the glory of my phoenix. I ran my fingers down the edges of my elephant's ears. The returning sunlight made them sing like crackling fire. I couldn't resist checking my pockets, just in case a flea had forgotten to leave. They were empty. I put my hands inside them just in case they could find something my eyes couldn't! My eyes were right; they had gone. I smiled.

'I didn't really want to keep them anyway. It isn't right to keep things that want to go.'

'You are wise, young lady.'

'I am?'

'Yes, life is about change, and if you cannot change you cannot take part in life.'

I sat watching the river beneath me as my elephant moved back through the grassier borders at the side of my river. I saw again the bluey-green dragonflies, darting from water lily to

45

bulrush. I smiled feeling again the quiver of his transparent wings at my neck.

The dragonflies were there and gone and we were at my mango tree. 'My mango tree!' I said, bouncing up and down with excitement at being back again. 'Do you think those little parrots are still fighting over the mangos?'

They were, indeed still there. My elephant kindly slowed as we passed them and my excitement took over as I waved and bounced and away flew a couple of these tiny parrots squawking hysterically. We stopped and my elephant took a mango from the tree. Again he lifted it over his head and squeezed the lovely sweet juice into my outstretched hands. I slurped it off my fingers and thumbs, giggling as I watched a very serious parrot argument, which left one parrot clinging upside down to a very thin branch. "He's going to fall and hurt himself!" I squealed watching fascinated.

'But his fall will turn to flight,' replied my elephant.

'Oh, yes, I'd forgotten he can fly!"

And as we walked away, that was just what he did! His wings stretched out till his downward fall became an arc returning him to a branch above his previous attackers, and the argument started all over again. My eyes didn't leave their colours till they vanished into the curtain of green that was my tree. Then it too, with its delicious fruit and fighting parrots, vanished into the distance of my jungle.

I sat licking the last of the mango's juice from my sticky hands. The jungle crowded the edges of my river. Bright red, blue and green streaks of much larger parrots kept screaming out of it, keeping me giggling at their acrobatics.

I recognised the path that had brought us down from the hospital. My elephant stopped. 'Do we have to leave?' I asked quietly not wanting to go.

No,' he replied.

'Oh, good! Are we going to go up my river now? Am I going to meet another of my animals?' I asked.

'You have met all the animals you need today.'

'Oh. So I don't have any more animals then.'

'These animals are your special animals. They all had something to teach you.'

'Yes, I know, but it's just that I only have seven animals. Couldn't I have some more?'

'Ah, I see. Look at it this way; the animals you've met today are important to you today. Tomorrow you will meet other animals that will teach you more of what you need to know. Each animal is unique and if you study them closely they can help you to understand who you are.'

'How can they do that?'

'Because those characteristics you see in them you can recognise in yourself.'

'But what about the phoenix?'

'What about the phoenix?'

'He can fly!'

'So?'

'But I can't fly, Mr Elephant!'

'Do you really believe you can't fly?'

'Well, I don't have his wings. How can I fly without wings?'

'Listen very carefully little one. Do you really believe there is anything you cannot do?'

I sat looking at the magical river beyond my elephant's head remembering all that lived beside it and my hand gently touched the gold on my elephant's ears. 'No, Mr Elephant, perhaps you're right. I don't think there is anything I can't do.'

'Tell me then how are you going to fly without wings?'

'I think I'll grow some.'

'And how do you know that you will be able to grow a pair of wings?' he asked.

'Because I can do anything, Mr Elephant.'

'You do know that you are a very wise young lady?'

'I am, aren't I?' I smiled a very confident smile.

'Now there is just one more thing we have to do.'

'What, Mr Elephant?'

'A bath!'

'Oh, no Mr Elephant, not another one! You've already given me lots and Mr

Panther's given me at least two!'

My elephant's golden trunk swung into action and I looked up watching the silver rain shoot above me. My eyes soon closed, expecting soon to be soaked, but this didn't happen. I felt just one drop fall on to my head and there it stayed. It sat in the hole in my head. The skin under it began to tingle, and then the droplet moved through the same skin and into the tube in my head. It began to move down the tube, leaving tingles as it fell. I could feel every inch of where it went. The tube took it down my neck, past my heart into my stomach, which was where the tube stopped.

But the silver droplet had other ideas. It kept going down through my legs and out of my feet, on to my elephant and into the river from whence it came.

As I felt the droplet leave my feet, the tingles left behind began to get bigger, spreading out and into the rest of my body. They got stronger and stronger until they reached the ends of my fingers and toes. I was humming all over with silver life. Gone was my river and the jungle at its edge. I was submersed in an energy of pure silver light. Feeling nothing but ripples of silver water running through me. I could not feel my elephant's trunk lift me from his back nor ever so gently lay me down....

As the last of the delicious silvery tingles slowed and left my body I began to feel what was around me. It wasn't my elephant. It felt more like sheets! 'Why am I back in bed Mr Elephant?' I said opening my eyes. But Mr Elephant had gone. I was back in my hospital bed, in a white room with a large window overlooking a sunlit lake.

I sat up and saw my mum sleeping on a chair.

'Hello Mum.' I said. She stirred a little. 'Mum!'

'Yes, darling?' she replied, not really awake yet.

I got out of bed and went over to her and shook her arm. 'Mum, wake up, I want to tell you about my elephant.' I climbed onto her lap as she really began to waken I started to talk.

'Do you remember the knocking on the door. Well it was an elephant. He was lovely. He's the animal of my heart. He lifted me onto his back 'cos he wanted to take me on a journey. Then we met a snake and he went inside of me here, past my heart, which really tickled, and out of my mouth, he then grew wings and flew away. Then we met a dragonfly. Why are you crying, Mum?'

'I'm just very glad you're back.'

'Of course I'm back! I did ask Mr Elephant if you could come too, but he said that it was my journey.'

'He did, did he?'

'Yes, he did say he'd bring me back and here I am. Are you sure you didn't know?'

'Yes, my darling! I always knew how strong you were.'

'That's what my panther said.'

'Your panther?'

'The Panther of my heart.'

'I thought you said you had an elephant at your heart?'

'Yes, I do. I have both. '

'Both?'

'Yes, the panther is the animal of the strength of my heart, you see!'

'Oh, dear, I think you've lost me there and I think you'd better get back into bed now.'

Mum lifted me down and I scrambled back into bed as a nurse came in. 'Hello

Sister, I wonder would you mind telling the doctors that she's awake.'

'Yes, of course. How are you feeling?' She lifted my pillow and tucked it in behind me then started straightening the sheets.

'I'm feeling fine thank you. Can I tell you about my elephant?'

'Your elephant?' The nurse looked at my Mum and they both started to laugh.

'I think we'll let the doctors have a look at you then you can tell us all about it. If you're not too tired that is. All right?'

'OK Mum.'

'All right chatterbox. Hush-up! I want a hug!' I hugged her, but not for long!

'Do you know what I'm going to do tomorrow?'

'No, do tell me.'

'I'm going to grow wings.'

'Are you indeed! You are clever! I don't think that I could grow wings!'

'Oh yes you can Mum. You can do anything you want to!'

And we did!

Further information about Jessica Clements' work

Jessica Clements has also taken her book, **"The Elephant of My Heart"** onto the stage as a children's show. As well as telling her story, Jessica also introduces the audience, young and old, to the Animal of their Hearts, in a short, guided visualisation.

Jessica Clements recorded further visualisations and these can be purchased from the website, www. animalofyourheart.co.uk or by emailing Jessica Clements at animalofyourheart@yahoo.co.uk

They can also be bought from Amazon MP3, Itunes.

They are: Animal of Your Heart Adult Visualisation
Animal of Your Heart Children's Visualisation
Animal of Your Heart Self-Healing Visualisation
Animal of Your Heart Conflict Resolution

These visualisations enable you, in a gentle and relaxed way, to continue to journey with your Heart's Animal in your own time. Suggestions about how to get the most out of using these visualisation techniques can be found on Jessica Clements' website www.animalofyourheart.co.uk

Further information about "Animal of Your Heart" workshops or upcoming performances of "The Elephant of My Heart" Children's Show can also be found on this website.

For Information on Deep Imagery

International Institute For Visualization Research
PO Box 632
Velarde NM 87582

www.deepimagery.org
www.facebook.com/deepimagery
IIVR@deepimagery.org

Eligio Stephen Gallegos, PhD,
PO Box 468
Velarde NM 87572

www.esgallegos.com
info@esgallegos.com

Books on Deep Imagery from Moon Bear Press:
Control and Obedience: The Human Illness
By E. S. Gallegos Ph.D (2014)

Chakra Power Animals: The Living Energies of the Chakras
By E. S. Gallegos Ph.D (2014)

Personal Totempole Process: Animal Imagery, the Chakras and Psychotherapy
By E. S. Gallegos Ph.D Kindle Edition (2012)

Animals of The Four Windows:
Integrating Thinking, Sensing, Feeling and Imagery
By E. S. Gallegos Ph.D. ISBN: 0944164404

Into Wholeness: The Path of Deep Imagery
By E. S. Gallegos Ph.D ISBN: 978-0944164228

Little Ed and Golden Bear
By E. S. Gallegos Ph.D. ISBN:978-0944164068

Simon McBride
Images & Cover Design
www.louisvmcbride.com